THE VICTORIA AND ALBERT COLOUR BOOKS

FIRST PUBLISHED IN GREAT BRITAIN 1989 BY
WEBB & BOWER (PUBLISHERS) LTD
9 COLLETON CRESCENT, EXETER, DEVON EX2 4BY
IN ASSOCIATION WITH MICHAEL JOSEPH LTD
27 WRIGHTS LANE, LONDON W8 5TZ
IN ASSOCIATION WITH THE VICTORIA AND ALBERT MUSEUM, LONDON

PENGUIN BOOKS LTD, REGISTERED OFFICES:
HARMONDSWORTH, MIDDLESEX, ENGLAND
PENGUIN BOOKS AUSTRALIA LTD, RINGWOOD, VICTORIA, AUSTRALIA
PENGUIN BOOKS CANADA LTD
2801 JOHN STREET, MARKHAM, ONTARIO, CANADA L3R 1D4
PENGUIN BOOKS (NZ) LTD, 182-190 WAIRAU ROAD, AUCKLAND 10, NEW ZEALAND

BOOK, COVER AND SLIPCASE DESIGN BY CARROLL, DEMPSEY & THIRKELL LTD

PRODUCTION BY NICK FACER/ROB KENDREW

COPYRIGHT © 1989 WEBB & BOWER (PUBLISHERS) LTD,
THE TRUSTEES OF THE VICTORIA AND ALBERT MUSEUM,
CARROLL, DEMPSEY & THIRKELL LTD

BRITISH LIBRARY CATALOGUING IN PUBLICATION DATA

VICTORIA AND ALBERT MUSEUM
IKATS - THE VICTORIA AND ALBERT COLOUR BOOKS SERIES 4
1. TEXTILES. IKAT. CATALOGUES, INDEXES
I. TITLE
746. 6′64

ISBN 0-86350-298-9

TYPESET IN GREAT BRITAIN BY OPTIC
COLOUR REPRODUCTION BY PENINSULAR REPRO SERVICE LTD
PRINTED AND BOUND IN HONG KONG

THE VICTORIA AND ALBERT COLOUR BOOKS

IKATS

INTRODUCTION BY
CLARE WOODTHORPE BROWNE

WEBB & BOWER
MICHAEL JOSEPH
MCMLXXXIX

THE TEXTILES illustrated in this book are a selection from the Victoria and Albert Museum's collection of nineteenth-century Central Asian ikats. Ikat is an Indonesian word, implying the act of tying or binding, and it is the technique of binding the yarn selectively before resist-dyeing that defines ikat cloth; but in practice it is the finished result, the beautiful soft blurring of edges in its patterns and the feathering of colours into each other that is ikat's immediately recognizable characteristic.

Ikat belongs in the textile traditions of such culturally and geographically separate parts of the world as Central America, the Ivory Coast of Africa and the Indonesian Archipelago; while the technique is widely practised it reaches its most sophisticated forms in Asia, particularly in Indonesia, Japan, India and Turkestan (throughout Asia, pattern and ornament are to a large extent produced by dyeing rather than weaving). The oldest known examples of ikat, surviving as fragments in the National Museum in Tokyo, are from the Asuka period of sixth- and seventh-century Japan; the production of *patola* (silk double ikat) in Gujarat, India, giving its name to the traditional wedding sari of the area, is thought to date from the fifth century AD and is still carried on today. The considerable beauty of ikat, and the status it possessed as a textile through the sophistication of its production, helped to ensure a continuation in the technique over centuries in many countries in Asia, and its diffusion and adoption in new cultures to which the trade routes carried it.

These ikats were acquired by the Victoria and Albert Museum in 1880.

7

They came as one collection of about fifty pieces, passed on to the Museum by the India Office; unfortunately no documentation has survived with them. When they were acquired they were all new pieces, thought to have come from one area and to be representative of the designs, colours and types of fabric in production at that time. Although they were brought to this country via Chinese Sinkiang Province, their provenance is almost certainly West (Russian) Turkestan, an area bordered in the north by the Aral Sea, in the west by the Caspian Sea, and reaching south to Iran and Afghanistan and east to China. It was an area exceptionally well rewarded by the benefits of lying on the Silk Route to the Far East; the meeting of different cultures through trade, as well as through more disruptive invasion and settlement, all contributed to a great wealth in its decorative arts. Among the most important centres of production were Bukhara, Samarkand and the Ferghana Valley. No central Asian ikats survive which can be positively dated before the late eighteenth century and the extraordinary skills of the Turkestan dyers and weavers of ikat were largely lost by the second decade of the twentieth; the nineteenth century saw the peak of their skills and this collection includes some exceptionally fine examples.

All these pieces are warp ikats (the pattern being dyed into the warp rather than the weft, or a combination of the two). They were woven either in pure silk, or with a silk warp and a heavy or fine cotton weft. The warp threads were tied in groups following a prearranged pattern with those sections on which the dye was not to take bound tightly with undyed cotton thread before the whole was dipped into a dyebath of the palest colour required. The warp threads would then be unbound, having taken the first colour in small sections along their length, retied in new places, and redyed in successively darker colours up to five times so that a maximum of six or, exceptionally, seven colours could be achieved. This was a very lengthy and labour intensive process and progressively added to the expense of the piece and its status as a luxury. Apart from indigo imported from India, and until the advent of synthetic colours in the late nineteenth century, dyes were made from plants locally available like madder to produce red, saffron and larkspur

for yellow, and the peel of pomegranates and the galls of pistachio trees for black. A stable green dye was hard to obtain and the colour was usually achieved by dyeing yellow onto blue. Many grad-ations in shades of purple, violet and pink could be obtained by dyeing red onto blue.

After the warp threads had been dyed they were spread out and untangled, then carefully laid on the loom. Shifting of the threads as they were wound on, as well as unevenness in the penetration of the dye under the edges of the resist-binding during the dyeing process, caused the character-istic blurring of lines and fusing or dovetailing of colours; this effect was exaggerated in pieces with less complicated designs by manipulating sections of the warp, creating stepped blocks or arrowheads, rather than depending entirely on the dyeing to create the pattern (*plate* 27). This technique became increasingly common towards the end of the nineteenth century, as did a falling away in the sophis-ticated palate of colours from natural dyes, competition from Russia in the market for cloth necessitating greater and greater economies in production (West Turkestan had become part of the Russian Empire shortly after 1865).

After weaving the cloth was sometimes folded repeatedly and beaten on a wooden block with a heavy mallet; this brought out the oils in the silk giving it a glazed finish (*plates* 7, 14). One piece might need the services of up to nine specialists, from spinning the silk through the stages of dyeing to weaving and finishing the cloth.

Silk and cotton ikats were woven in strips of 45.75 cms (18″) or less and then sewn together in panels to create either furnishings such as wall-hangings and bedcovers or clothing for men, women and children. The most common garment was the *chapan*; this type of coat was worn by all classes, but with the type of cloth used in its construction strictly regulated to denote the rank of the wearer or the occasion (garments inappropriately grand could be confiscated or more serious penalties enforced). It was long, sometimes reaching to the ground, and could be worn loose or belted; it was frequently padded or quilted for warmth and cut with sleeves long enough for the hands to be withdrawn inside. This also complied with an Islamic convention in dress that no part of the body should be uncovered. There were no pockets; a bag hung from the belt would serve instead. Ikat was used for the linings of the gold brocade *chalats* (ceremonial coats) of the highest ranking dignitaries, and for the everyday wear of merchants and all men of wealth and rank; for poorer people it was kept for festivity and celebration. Ikat *chalats* were bestowed as marks of distinction and gratitude, and often worn, draped over the shoulders as many as six at a time, as a display of prestige.

The luxuriousness of the cloth demanded economical use of panelling and patching in the construction of the coats. They were cut along straight and diagonal lines, with main seams along the selvedges so that nothing was wasted, and anything left used for the facings and gussets. The apparently random joining of patterns and juxtaposition of pattern flows brought about a deliberate emphasis of the visual impact of the garment – with little variation in the cut of the *chapan* variety had to be created in colour and pattern.

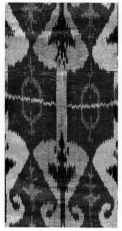

Islamic laws governing dress affected the composition of the ikat cloth used for clothing; pure silk with its connotations of luxury and indulgence was forbidden to men (although this injunction did not apply to women) and so a cotton weft was incorporated. This mixed fabric known as *mesru* (permitted), was both luxurious and within the law, and was used for the majority of the pieces in this collection.

Patterns created in the ikats sometimes incorporated clearly or less clearly recognizable motifs, and sometimes were purely abstract. The motifs could be day to day objects or symbolic of some aspect of life; the examples in this book include cypress trees representing the Tree of Life (*plates* 10, 12), pomegranates (*plate* 3) rams' horns (*plate* 25), tulips (*plate* 6), and the comb-like motif known as the Hand of Fatima, daughter of the Prophet. The designers had the potential resources of all the different cultural and religious imagery of the many peoples converging on this part of Central Asia, and for all those motifs like the tulip familiar from Turkish and Persian art there are as many with unknown origin or symbolism. There was also, naturally, a borrowing of design elements from other textile arts. The palate of background colours in many of these ikats evokes the grounds of Turkoman carpets; some of the highly stylized motifs can be identified from their more familiar representation in the *suzani* embroideries of the area. The images can be stylized almost out of recognition; possibly the designers were influenced by Islamic proscriptions against representations of living forms, possibly they were just experimenting with shapes and creating symmetry. Mirror images were produced by folding over the warp threads before binding and dyeing so that identical colours were picked up on either side (this produced the characteristic wavy white line (*plate* 17) where the threads were tied) and the whole effect of the pattern could be emphasized in the piecing together of the panels for the creation of a garment or hanging.

Turkestan ikats are of great interest as the product of so many cultural influences and reinterpretation and development of traditional skills but they are most outstanding for their sheer visual impact, their stunning colours and patterns, and the extraordinary, subtle blurring and shifting of their shapes and lines; this collection presents a wide cross-section of their range and beauty.

I am grateful to Jennifer Wearden for her advice and encouragement in my research on this collection.   *Clare Woodthorpe Browne*

BIBLIOGRAPHY

Goldman, Shaffer and Marechal, *Central Asian Textiles: Ikat* (Hali. Issue 27, London 1985)

Exhibition catalogue *Ikats: Woven Silks from Central Asia, The Rau Collection* (Basil Blackwell in association with the Crafts Council, Oxford, 1988)

Kalter, Johannes *The Arts and Crafts of Turkestan* (Thames and Hudson, London, 1984)

Leix, A *Turkestan and its Textile Crafts* (CIBA Review No 40, Basle, 1941)

Lennor Larsen, Jack *The Dyer's Art: Ikat, Batik, Plangi* (Van Nostrand/Reinhold, New York, 1976)

THE PLATES

1

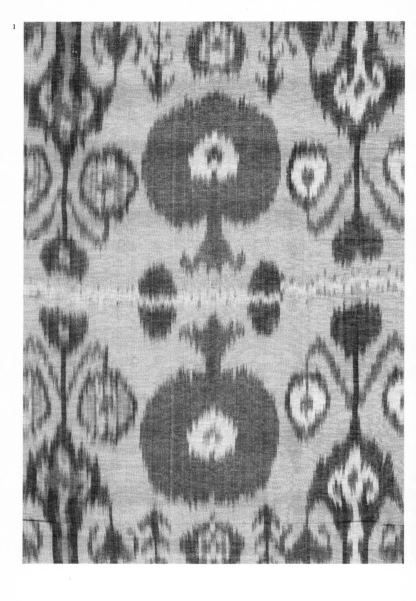

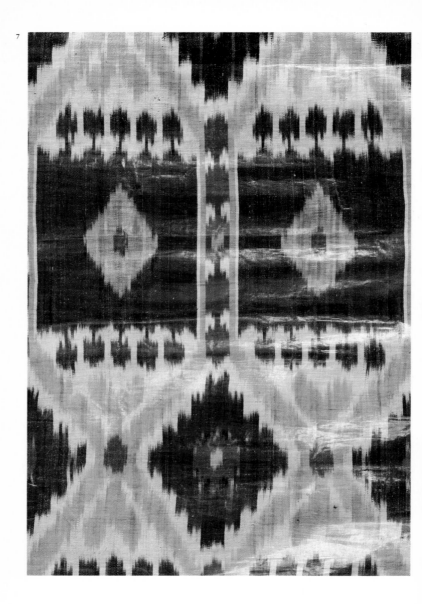

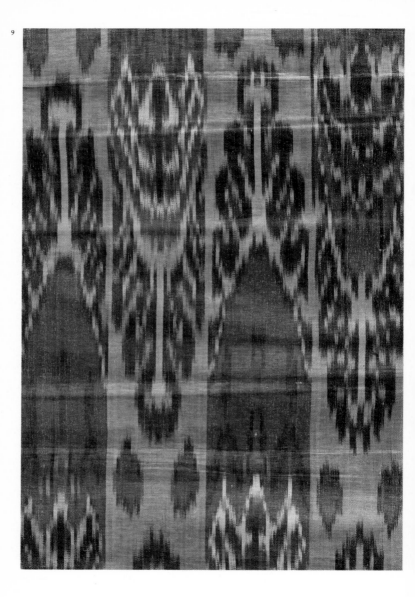

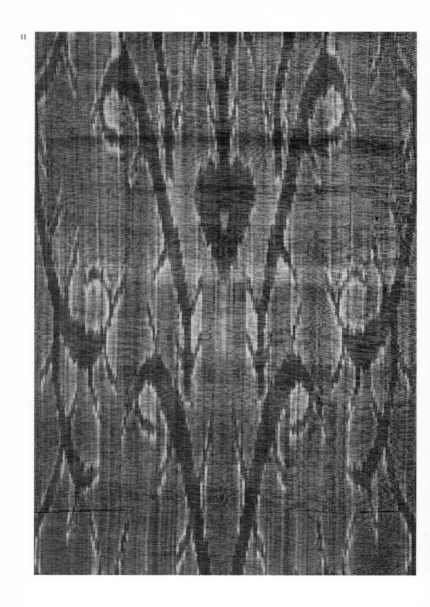

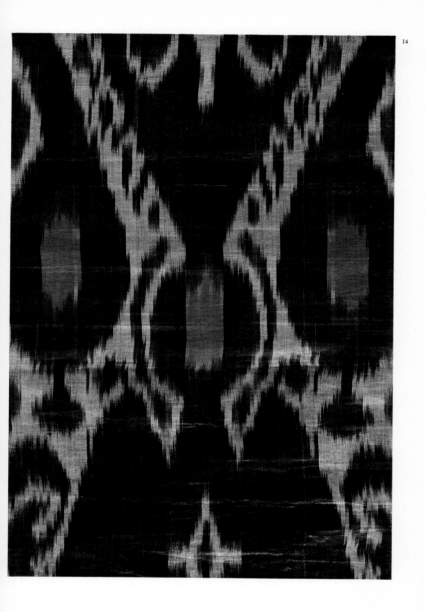

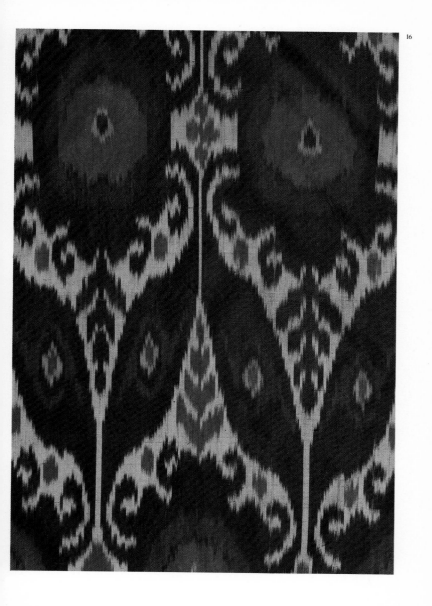

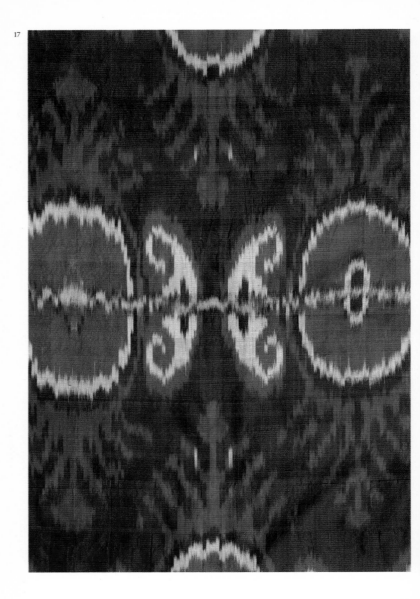

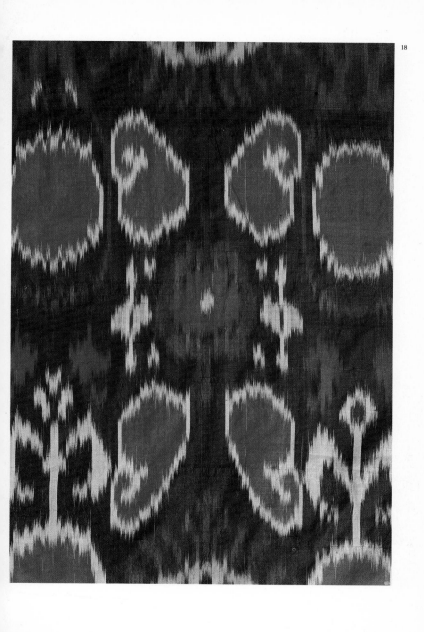

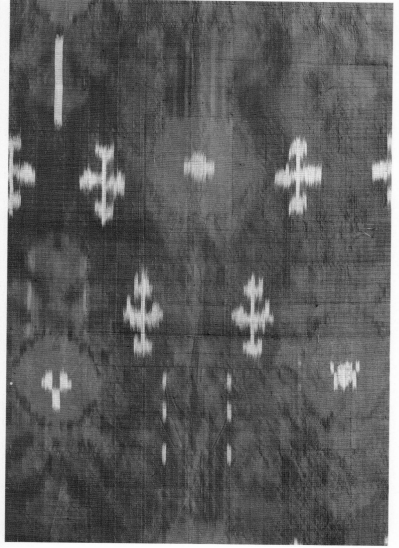

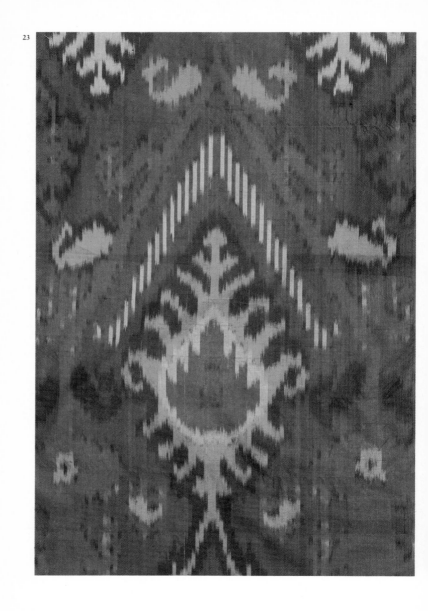

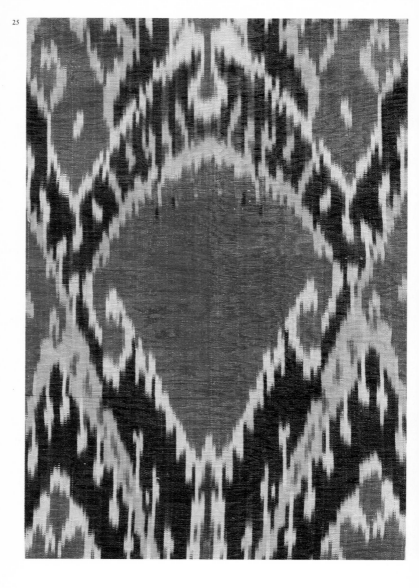

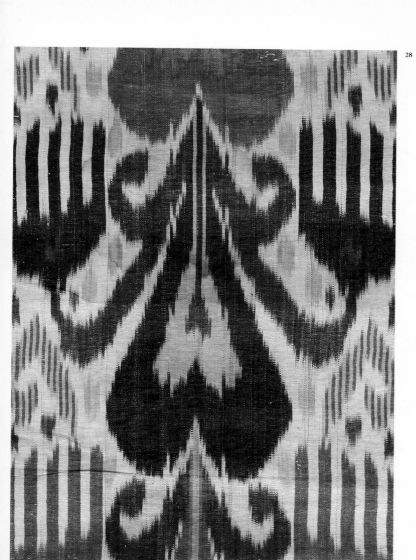

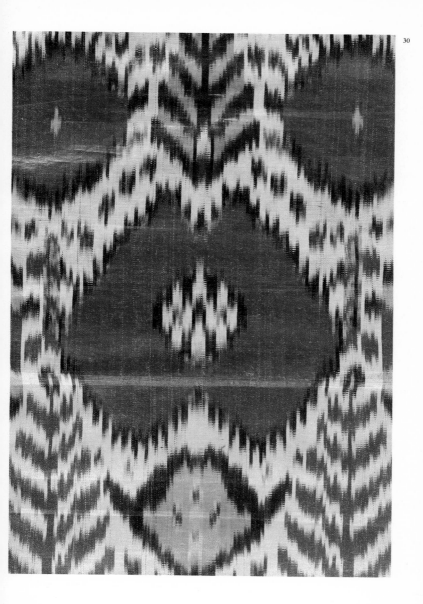

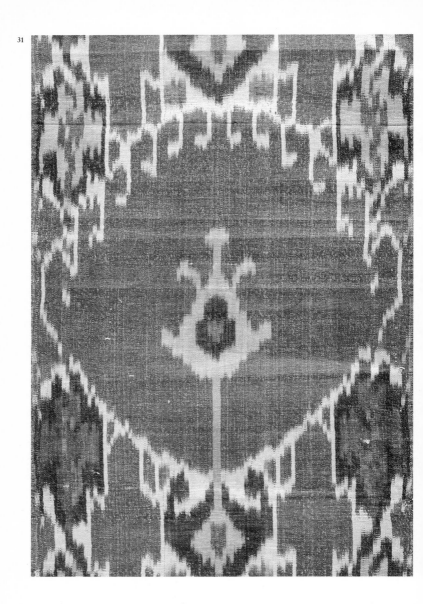

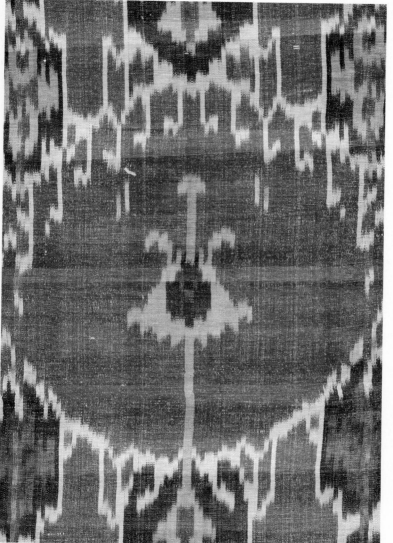

THE
VICTORIA
& ALBERT
COLOUR
BOOKS